Twenty to Make

Felt Christmas Decorations

Corinne Lapierre

Windsor and Maidenhead

First published in Great Britain 2013

Search Press Limited
Wellwood, North Farm Road,
Tunbridge Wells, Kent TN2 3DR

Text copyright © Corinne Lapierre 2013

Photographs by Paul Bricknell at
Search Press Studios

Photographs and design copyright
© Search Press Ltd 2013

Print ISBN: 978-1-84448-943-5
Epub ISBN: 978-1-78126-181-1
Mobi ISBN: 978-1-78126-182-8
PDF ISBN: 978-1-78126-183-5

Suppliers
If you have difficulty in obtaining any of the
materials and equipment mentioned in this
book, then please visit the Search Press website
for details of suppliers: www.searchpress.com

Printed in China

Dedication
*To my three little pixies, Emily, Oscar and
Thomas, who always put the magic
into Christmas!*

Acknowledgements
Thanks to Katie French for asking me to
write this book in the first place and for her
gentle guidance.
Thank you to everyone who listened to me
talking about this book for hours and shared
my excitement: Mike, Emma, Fabienne and
the studio crew.
Last but not least, thank you to my lovely
family who always believes in me and gives
me so much support!

Contents

Introduction

I stumbled across felt a few years ago and soon became hooked. Felt is one of the oldest textiles known to man, traditionally made from wool. It is the only non-woven fabric and for this reason it displays unique qualities, the main one being that it does not fray. You can, of course, buy synthetic craft felt, but it is so much more special to use wool felt, or at least a wool-mix felt. You can simply put your old woolly sweaters in the washing machine and you will have felt! All the projects in this book have been made with wool felt, and the stocking on pages 14–15 was made with hand-rolled felt for a truly luxurious feel.

The pre-Christmas season is always so special. With the nights drawing in, it is the perfect time to make decorations and gifts. Most of these projects are very simple and can be made in one sitting. Some might require a little bit more time, like the advent garland (see pages 36–37), but all can easily be made while sitting in a comfortable chair in front of the fire.

I wanted all my projects to look fresh and modern, so (apart from the gingerbread men!) I used a gentle palette of muted grey, green, red, white and pale blue to give them a Scandinavian feel, but if you prefer a more traditional look simply change the colours to bright greens, reds and golds.

It has been such a treat to write this book; my only wish is that you have as much fun making these projects as I had.

Enjoy!

Christmas Pixie

Materials:

42 x 45cm (16½ x 17¾in) of red felt

10 x 10cm (4 x 4in) of flesh-coloured felt

3 x 3cm (1¼ x 1¼in) of white felt per button

30cm (11¾in) of red checkered ribbon, approximately 2cm (¾in) wide

Red and brown or black embroidery cotton

10 x 10cm (4 x 4in) of medium-weight fusible bonding material

About 30g (1oz) of toy filling

Tools:

Paper and fabric scissors

Dressmaking pins

Pencil

Embroidery needle

Iron

Sewing machine (optional)

Instructions:

1 Enlarge the templates on page 48 and cut them out. Transfer the body outline to the red felt and cut out two bodies. Cut one face from the flesh-coloured felt and one from the bonding material. Cut as many buttons as you wish. I have used three.

2 On the face, draw the features using a very faint pencil line. Think of the expression you want your pixie to have. Embroider on the features using back stitch.

3 Iron the bonding material on to the back of the felt face. Leave to cool and peel off the backing paper. Place on top of the front body piece, using the picture as guidance, and iron it in place following the manufacturer's instructions.

4 Tie the ribbon into a bow and trim the ends at an angle. Attach the bow to the pixie's head with a couple of stitches.

5 Sew the buttons down the front of the body with a single large cross stitch.

6 To assemble the body, use either machine or hand stitching. If you are using hand stitching, place the front on to the back piece, wrong sides together, and sew all the way round with a blanket or overhand stitch. Leave a small gap of around 10cm (4in) at the bottom and stuff the pixie with toy filling before closing the gap completely.

If you are using a sewing machine, place the front on to the back piece, right sides together. Stitch all the way round leaving a gap at the bottom of about 10cm (4in). Use a medium straight stitch worked 0.5cm (¼in) from the edge. Turn the pixie right side out and stuff with the toy stuffing. Close the gap with a small overhand stitch.

This pixie's beauty lies in its simplicity but you could add more details if you wish. You could decorate the hood with stitching or beads. Use real buttons instead of the felt ones or cut felt flower shapes to sew on the coat.

Embroidery Hoops

Materials:

Mini wooden embroidery hoops, 7.5 or
    10cm (3 or 4in) are ideal

12 x 12cm (4¾ x 4¾in) of felt per hoop

Contrasting embroidery cotton

16cm (6¼in) of hessian string or
    fine ribbon per hoop

Tools:

Fabric and
    embroidery scissors

Embroidery needle

Chalk

Pencil

Instructions:

1 Place an embroidery hoop on top of a piece of felt and
draw around it with a very faint chalk line. Remove the
hoop and cut your felt about 0.5cm (¼in) bigger than the
chalk circle.

2 On the clean side of the felt, draw the pattern you wish to
embroider using a very faint pencil line. It is much easier if you
find the centre first by folding your circle in half and half again.
Either follow the pictures for guidance or create your own pattern.
It could be something very simple like lines crossing in the centre to
form a star.

3 When you are satisfied with your design, open the embroidery
hoop by unscrewing the tightening screw and place your felt (design
side up) on top of the inner hoop as centred as possible. Place the
outer hoop on top with the tightening screw at the top. Push it
down to fit around the inner hoop and trapping the felt in between.
Make sure the felt is stretched evenly and tighten up the screw to
hold it in place.

4 You can now embroider your design following your pencil
drawing. Use only two or three strands of embroidery cotton to
achieve finer results. Simple stitches such as back stitch, fly stitch
and French knots can be very effective.

5 Thread a piece of hessian string or fine ribbon into the tightening
screw and tie a knot to make a hanging loop.

Instead of a pattern you could embroider a special word that is meaningful to you or a name with a date. This will make a lovely present for a baby's first Christmas.

Festive Wreath

Materials:

1 plain willow wreath

20 x 20cm (7¾ x 7¾in) of green felt

7 x 12cm (2¾ x 4¾in) of red felt

13 x 9cm (5 x 3½in) of brown felt

Fabric glue

Embroidery cotton in red and brown

2 small round black beads

About 5g (¼oz) of toy filling

30cm (11¾in) of red checkered ribbon,
approximately 2cm (¾in) wide

Tools:

Paper, fabric and embroidery scissors

Pencil

Dressmaking pins

Beading needle

Embroidery needle

Instructions:

1 Enlarge the templates on page 47 and cut them out. Transfer the shapes to the felt so that you have six green holly leaves, three red berries and, for the bird, two brown upper pieces and two red lower pieces. Cut out the felt with fabric scissors.

2 Start by making the robin: place a brown body piece on top of a red one and slightly overlap them by about 1cm (½in). Stitch them in place with a small overhand stitch. Do this for the other two body pieces. You should now have two pieces that each look like a bird.

3 On each piece, place a bead where the eye should be and attach it securely with a couple of stitches.

4 Place the two pieces together, wrong sides facing. Starting from the tail end, sew the front and back together with a blanket or overhand stitch. When you have stitched about three-quarters of the way round, stuff the bird with the toy filling, using the ends of your scissors

to push the filling in if needed. Close the bird completely and secure the stitching with a knot.

5 To make the holly leaves, thread your needle with red cotton. Place a red circle on top of the base of a leaf and secure in place with a simple stitch. Place another leaf facing the first one with its base underneath. Sew it in place with a couple of stitches. Repeat to make three sets of holly leaves.

6 Take your wreath and decide which is the top. Thread your ribbon through the willow at the top and tie a knot. This will be your hanging loop.

7 Place your holly leaves and the robin where you want them and attach them to the wreath with a little bit of fabric glue on the back of your felt. Press down gently for a few seconds. You might have to push the robin in between the willow slightly to hold it firmly. Add a little bit more glue if necessary.

You could use a few leaves of real holly to decorate your wreath. Add a few shiny red beads glued on to the red felt berries and perhaps a few small frosted glass ones on the edges of the felt leaves to give the wreath a truly wintry feel.

Bird of Peace

Materials:

2 pieces of white felt, 10 x 10cm (4 x 4in)

6 x 10cm (2¼ x 4in) of pale blue felt

Red and white embroidery cotton

2 or 3 red glass beads

About 3g (⅛oz) of toy filling

Tools:

Paper, fabric and embroidery scissors

Dressmaking pins

Pencil

Embroidery needle

Instructions:

1 Enlarge the templates on page 48 and cut them out. Transfer the shapes to the felt and cut two white circles and two blue pieces for the bird. When cutting out the inner circle of the white felt, use very sharp-pointed scissors. Embroidery scissors are perfect for this.

2 With a very faint pencil line, draw the wings on the bird's front and back. Embroider them on with a back stitch. Make each eye with a simple French knot.

3 Place the front and back pieces together, wrong sides facing, and sew them together with a blanket or overhand stitch. Stuff the bird with the filling before closing completely.

4 Draw a circle with a faint pencil line on your white felt and embroider along it with back stitch. When you have completed the circle, add small stitches at regular intervals to look like little stems.

5 Stitch the two circles together using the white cotton and a small overhand stitch on the outer and inner edges.

6 Thread your needle with the red cotton using the full thickness of thread. Take the needle through the inner edge of the white circle and pull the thread through leaving a short tail. Catch a tiny bit of felt and a white stitch to make a knot. Trim the end of the thread and push it in between the two layers of felt to hide it.

7 Pass the needle up through the base of the bird and out through the centre of the back. Use the picture for guidance. Thread on a bead and knot the thread to hold it in place. Make another knot about 1cm (½in) higher and thread on another bead. Pass the needle up through the top of the white circle, between the two layers of felt. At this point, make sure your thread is lying in a straight line, otherwise your bird will hang crooked. Be careful not to pull too tightly on the thread or the circle could easily become an oval!

8 Add another bead at the top of the circle if you wish. Make a hanging loop with your thread, push the needle back into the felt and tie a knot. Trim the end of the cotton and hide the loose end in between the felt layers.

You could make a bigger version of this decoration by simply enlarging the templates. Try hanging it on your wall, your door or in a window for an eye-catching statement piece. You may need to fill the white circle with toy stuffing to give it more stability.

Christmas Stocking

Materials:

30 x 50cm (11¾ x 19¾in) of green felt

20 x 25cm (7¾ x 9¾in) of red felt

20 x 20cm (7¾ x 7¾ in) of polka dot cotton
fabric for the lining

54cm (21¼in) of narrow green ribbon

Red and green embroidery cotton

Tools:

Paper, fabric and embroidery scissors

Pencil, paper, ruler and pair of compasses

Dressmaking pins

Embroidery needle

Iron

Sewing machine (optional)

Instructions:

1 Enlarge the template on page 46 and cut it out. Transfer the shape to the green felt and cut two pieces for the front and back of the stocking.

2 On the piece of paper draw an 17 x 9cm (6¾ x 3½in) rectangle and a circle of 6cm (2¼in) diameter. Cut them out and transfer them to the red felt. Cut two rectangles and three circles. Cut two rectangles from the polka dot fabric too.

3 To resemble buttons, sew the circles down the side of the stocking front using a very large cross stitch worked with the thread doubled.

4 Cut the ribbon in three pieces of length 18cm (7in). Place two of these pieces on one of the red rectangles, approximately 2cm (¾in) away from one of the long edges. See the picture for guidance. Pin then stitch the ribbon in place with a small running stitch along the centre. You can do this with a sewing machine if you wish.

5 Place this rectangle on top of the stocking front (with the buttons), right sides together, and align the ribboned edge with the top edge of the stocking. Stitch them together with a back stitch, 1cm (½in) from the edge. Iron the seam flat.

6 Repeat step 5 with the back pieces, which are left plain. Ensure that both the front and back pieces will face the same direction when assembled!

7 Place and pin the front stocking on top of the back one, wrong sides together, and sew them together with a blanket stitch all the way round, except for the opening at the top. If you prefer, use a sewing machine: place the pieces right sides together and stitch with a medium straight stitch, 1cm (½in) from the edge. Turn your stocking right side out, making sure the point is pushed out all the way.

8 Place your two pieces of polka dot fabric right sides together and stitch 1cm (½in) from the edge on both short sides. You can do this by hand with a back stitch or with a sewing machine.

9 With your stocking right side out, place the lining, wrong side out, around the red cuff. Align the top edges and the side seams. Sew them together 1cm (½in) from the edge.

10 Fold the lining over on to the inside of the stocking and iron. Pay special attention to the top edge to make sure it lies flat and straight.

11 With the lining inside, stitch the loose edge on to the inside seam of the cuff (where the red felt is sewn to the green), turning the raw edge under as you work. Use a small straight stitch, making sure it does not show on the right side.

12 Attach the last piece of ribbon, folded in half to make a hanging loop. Use a few strong stitches on the inside of the stocking.

This stocking will last for years and become a real family heirloom. Why not make it even more special by personalising it? Simply embroider the name of the child on the top cuff with a back stitch.

Little Reindeer

Materials:

20 x 20cm (7¾ x 7¾in) of red felt

White embroidery cotton

About 7g (¼oz) of toy filling

Tools:

Paper, fabric and embroidery scissors

Dressmaking pins

Pencil

Embroidery needle

Instructions:

1 Enlarge the templates on page 47 and cut them out. Transfer the shapes to the felt and cut two bodies and one tummy. To cut around the antlers, use small, pointed scissors such as embroidery scissors.

2 On each body piece draw a little circle on the side using a faint pencil line, about 2cm (¾in) in diameter. Embroider along the line with back stitch, adding some little straight stitches all the way round to look like tiny stems. You can add French knots too if you wish. Embroider the eyes using little French knots.

3 Fold the tummy piece in half with the legs matching. Pin or mark each end of the fold line with a pencil. Place the folded tummy piece on top of a body piece, wrong sides together, ensuring the legs match perfectly. Stitch them together with a small overhand stitch, working round from the front to the back, starting and finishing at the fold line. Do not cut your thread.

4 Now place the front piece on top, matching the legs again, and carry on stitching until you are back to where you started at the front.

5 At this point it is a good idea to start stuffing the legs of the reindeer. Push the filling into the legs with a pencil.

6 Sew the back of the reindeer, starting from the point where you stopped stitching at the front and continuing around the head and the antlers and along the back. Fill the reindeer with the stuffing as you go along. Do not worry too much about filling the antlers. End your stitching at the back with a little knot.

Christmas Place Setting

Materials:
25 x 15cm (9¾ x 6in) of grey felt
10 x 10cm (4 x 4in) of white felt
60cm (23½in) of red ric-rac
Red embroidery cotton

Tools:
Paper, fabric and embroidery scissors
Zigzag scissors
Dressmaking pins
Embroidery needle
Pencil, ruler and pair of compasses
Paper
Fabric glue

Instructions:

1 On your piece of paper draw a 10 x 15cm (4 x 6in) rectangle, a 15 x 5cm (6 x 2in) rectangle and two circles of 6cm (2¼in) and 3cm (1¼in) diameter. Cut out these templates and transfer them to the felt. Cut two large rectangles and one small rectangle from the grey felt, and one circle of each size from the white felt using the zigzag scissors.

2 For the cutlery pouch, place the large circle on one of the large rectangles, roughly in the middle. Starting from the centre of the circle and going through both layers, make a cross (+) using long straight stitches and then an x shape. This will make a lovely star. Add a French knot at the end of each stitch, leaving a small gap.

3 Place a thin line of fabric glue about 1.5cm (¾in) from the top edge, and another one 1.5cm (¾in) from the bottom edge of the felt rectangle. Stick on the ric-rac by pressing it down firmly for a few seconds. Leave about 1cm (½in) of ric-rac sticking out at the sides.

4 Place this grey rectangle on top of the other one, wrong sides together, and sew them together on three sides with a blanket stitch. Leave the top open. Tuck the ends of the ric-rac inside as you stitch for a clean finish.

5 For the napkin ring, place the small circle in the middle of the small rectangle of felt and repeat step 2 for the stitching.

6 Repeat step 3 to attach the ric-rac close to the long edges.

7 Close the napkin ring at the back by overlapping it slightly and sewing together with a few cross stitches.

This set looks stylish with a very simple embroidered design. If you are feeling more confident with your embroidery, try stitching a more intricate design or create a unique family monogram.

Gingerbread House

Materials:

40 x 15cm (15¾ x 6in) of light blue felt

8 x 5cm (3¼ x 2in) of white felt

2 pieces of red felt: 16 x 14cm (6¼ x 5½in) for the roof and 3 x 3cm (1¼ x 1¼in) for the heart

30 x 40cm (11¾ x 15¾in) of thick cream felt

35 x 40cm (13¾ x 15¾in) of heavy-weight fusible bonding material

Red embroidery cotton

25cm (9¾in) of red ric-rac, and 35cm (13¾in) of white ric-rac cut in half

Fabric glue

Tools:

Paper, fabric and embroidery scissors

Embroidery needle

Dressmaking pins

Paper

Pencil and ruler

Ruler

Iron

Instructions:

1 On the piece of paper, draw and cut out: one rectangle measuring 8 x 15cm (3¼ x 6in) for the two long walls and the base (A); one rectangle measuring 16 x 7cm (6¼ x 2¾in) for the roof (B); and one rectangle measuring 8 x 12cm (3¼ x 4¾in) for the sides (C). Place C with the long edges vertical, and mark the middle of the top edge. Measure 4cm (1½in) down from the top on each side of the rectangle. Link these points to the centre top to create the roof shape. For the door, draw and cut out a rectangle measuring 4 x 3cm (1½ x 1¼in) (D), and for the windows draw a 2.5 x 2.5cm (¾ x ¾in) square (E).

2 Iron the fusible bonding material on to the pieces of light blue, red and white felt. Using

your templates cut: from the blue felt, three pieces of A and two of C; from the large piece of red felt, two pieces of B; from the white felt, one piece of D and four of E.

3 Peel off the paper backing and place pieces A, B and C on to the thick cream felt, sticky side down. Iron to bond the fabrics together and trim to shape.

4 Take your four walls (2 x A and 2 x C) and position the windows (E) and the door (D). Follow the picture for guidance. Iron to bond them to the house. On the windows make a cross with a thin line of glue and stick on the red ric-rac, trimmed to size.

5 Enlarge the heart template on page 47, cut it out and transfer it to the small piece of red felt. Cut it out and iron it on to the door. Alternatively, add a small button or bead to the door.

6 Sew the edges of all four walls together with overhand or blanket stitch to build the house. Sew the base to the walls in the same way.

7 Sew the two roof pieces together along the apex with overhand or blanket stitch.

8 Draw a thin line of glue just above the bottom edge on each side of the roof and stick on the white ric-rac.

9 Open up the roof and rest it on top of the house.

Instead of using light blue and red, you could use more traditional gingerbread colours such as brown and white and decorate it with coloured ribbons, buttons and beads. You could also personalise this house with a name or number and other finishing touches – the perfect gift to welcome someone to their new home!

Sweet Christmas Trees

Materials:

15 x 12cm (6 x 4¾in) of white or green felt for
the tree

3 x 3cm (1¼ x 1¼in) of red or brown felt for
the trunk

Red ric-rac or narrow ribbon

10–12 small buttons, beads or sequins

Silver embroidery cotton

About 5g (¼oz) of toy filling

Tools:

Paper, fabric and embroidery scissors

Embroidery needle

Dressmaking pins

Fabric glue

Instructions:

1 Enlarge the templates on page 47 and cut
them out. Transfer them to the felt and cut two
pieces for the tree and two for the trunk.

2 Sew the trunk pieces together, leaving the
top open, using just two or three strands of
silver embroidery cotton. Stuff with a little bit of
toy filling.

3 For the tree with baubles, sew the buttons,
beads or sequins all over the tree. You can
decorate either the front only or the front and
the back. Do not decorate the tree with the
garland until after you have stitched the front
and the back together.

4 Take a 15–20cm (6–7¾in) length of silver
embroidery thread and fold it in half. This will
be the hanging loop. Knot the ends and place
on the wrong side of the back of the tree, at
the top. Make a couple of small stitches using
two or three strands of cotton to secure it in
place. Do not cut your thread. Simply place the
front piece on top of the back piece, wrong
sides together, with the ends of the hanging
loop sandwiched between and, using overhand
stitch, sew all the way around the edge to
the bottom of the tree. Insert the trunk, and

stitch through the tree and the trunk to hold
it securely. Carry on stitching back to the top
of the tree. Fill your tree with stuffing before
closing it completely.

5 For the tree with the garland, place a little
dab of fabric glue at the top of the tree and
attach one end of the ric-rac or ribbon. Wrap
the length of ric-rac or ribbon all around the
tree, working down towards the bottom. Glue
the other end just above the trunk, trimming
the ribbon off neatly. You may want to add a
few drops of glue here and there to hold the
ric-rac in position.

You could make a few trees and hang them all on a piece of string to make a very festive bunting!

Gift Tags

Materials:

2 pieces of felt: 5 x 9cm (2 x 3½in) per tag.
I used red and cream for one tag and blue and cream for the other

Scraps of felt, ribbon and small buttons or beads

12cm (4¾in) of narrow ribbon per tag

Contrasting embroidery cotton

Fabric glue

Tools:

Paper, fabric and embroidery scissors

Zigzag scissors

Embroidery needle

Paper

Pencil and ruler

Instructions:

1 On the piece of paper, draw a 9 x 5cm (3½ x 2in) rectangle. Make a mark 1cm (½in) from each corner and cut off the corners either in a straight line or curved. This will be the template for your tags.

2 Transfer the template to the felt and cut two different-coloured pieces per tag.

For the red tag:

3 Cut a 2 x 4cm (¾ x 1½in) rectangle of felt in a contrasting colour using zigzag scissors. Write the name you wish to embroider on it with a faint pencil line. Embroider the name using back stitch. Place this name piece on top of the red rectangle and attach it with French knots in each corner.

4 Place the red rectangle on top of the cream rectangle. Take the 12cm (4¾in) of ribbon, fold it in half and sandwich the looped end in between the two rectangles, half way along one of the short edges. Sew the sides of the tag together with blanket stitch, matching the two rectangles perfectly and ensuring the looped ribbon is held securely in place.

For the blue tag:

5 Write the name in the centre of the blue rectangle with a faint pencil line. Embroider it with back stitch.

6 With the fabric glue, draw a horizontal line above and below the name, approximately 1cm (½in) from each edge. Place your decorative ribbon on it and trim it off neatly at the edges. Repeat with the two vertical lines of ribbon on each side of the name.

7 Place a dot of glue on each corner where the two ribbons cross and stick on a small button.

8 When dry, apply glue very thinly to the back of your blue felt rectangle, leave it to touch dry and place it on top of the cream rectangle. Press them firmly together for a few seconds, wiping away any glue which may seep out.

9 Thread your 12cm (4¾in) length of ribbon through a very large embroidery needle and push it through the two layers of felt to create the tie. Secure it to the tag with a knot.

These gift tags will make any present really special and can be used as a key ring or as a door sign by the recipient of your gift. They can also be tied on to school bags, overnight bags, sports bags, lunch boxes or small storage baskets.

Gingerbread Men

Materials:

For a garland of four gingerbread men:

2 pieces of felt: 13 x 11cm (5 x 4¼in) per gingerbread man; use a different shade of brown for each figure

6 small beads

30cm (11¾in) of white 6mm (¼in) ric-rac per figure

40cm (15¾in) of 6–9mm (¼–½in) wide gingham ribbon per figure

80cm (31½in) of narrow ribbon or string

Brown and red embroidery cotton

About 20g (¾oz) of toy filling

Tools:

Paper, fabric and embroidery scissors

Pencil

Embroidery needle

Beading needle

Dressmaking pins

Instructions:

1 Enlarge the template on page 47 and cut it out. Transfer the outline to the felt to cut two body pieces per gingerbread man.

2 For each figure, draw the face on one body piece. Think carefully about the expression you wish your gingerbread man to have. Semi-circles are great for smiley or sleepy eyes, or small cross stitches also work well. Embroider the features on using back stitch.

3 Sew three beads down the front of two of your gingerbread men as buttons.

4 Use the ric-rac to decorate the other two figures as you would use icing on a gingerbread man biscuit. Place small pieces on the body front to make cuffs around the arms and legs or the hem of a skirt. Cut the pieces of ric-rac slightly bigger than needed so that you can fold the edges underneath to keep them neat. Secure the ric-rac in place at the edges with very small stitches.

5 Use the gingham ribbon to make a scarf or a tie. Simply knot it at the front or tie it in a bow.

6 Lay all of the back pieces in a row, right side down, in the order in which they will be strung on the garland and approximately 5cm (2in) apart. Lay the ribbon or string across them, level with the ends of the arms. For each figure, place the front piece on top of the back piece, wrong sides facing, and pin them together, ensuring that the ribbon is held in place securely.

7 Stitch the first figure together with blanket or overhand stitch, making sure you stitch around and not through the ribbon at the ends of the arms. This will hold the gingerbread man in place, but still allow him to be moved along the ribbon if necessary. When you get to the ric-rac edges, make sure they are folded neatly inside and secure. Leave a small gap for stuffing.

8 Fill your gingerbread man with the stuffing and close the seam completely. Repeat for all of the gingerbread men.

You could string your gingerbread men vertically instead of horizontally and hang them from a door handle, for example. Simply pass the ribbon through from the tops of their heads to between their legs. You could also create individual hanging decorations. For the hanging loops, cut a piece of ribbon to about 20cm (7¾in) and fold it in half to form a loop. Attach it at the top of the head, hiding the ends of the loop inside.

Christmas Card String

Materials:

For each stocking:
1 piece of pale blue or green felt
    5 x 4.5cm (2 x 1¾in)
2 or 3 mini buttons, or 3cm (1¼in) of
    ric-rac or mini pompom trim

For each candy cane:
1 piece of white felt 5 x 3cm (2 x 1¼in)
80cm (31½in) of 3mm (⅛in) wide red satin ribbon

1.5m (60in) of hessian string

10 wooden clothes pegs

Fabric glue

Medium-weight fusible bonding material

Tools:

Paper and fabric scissors

Pencil

Iron

Instructions:

1 Iron the fusible bonding material on to the pieces of felt following the manufacturer's instructions. Leave to cool. The fusible bonding material will stiffen the felt and keep it in shape.

2 Enlarge the templates on page 48 and cut them out. For each shape, place the template on the back of the felt prepared in step 1 (the paper side) and draw around it with a pencil. Make five stockings and five candy canes. Cut out the felt with the fabric scissors.

For the candy canes:
3 Put a little bit of glue on the back at the bottom and attach the end of the red satin ribbon. Wrap the ribbon around the cane all the way to the top. Cut the ribbon, fold the end on to the back of the top of the candy cane. Leave to dry.

For the stockings:
4 Stick a little piece of ric-rac or pompom trim around the top by placing a little dab of glue on the back, or simply stick the mini buttons down one side on the front.

5 Line up all your wooden pegs and place a little dab of glue on the top part of one. Place a candy cane or stocking on it, pressing firmly for a few seconds. Repeat for all the pegs. Leave them to dry thoroughly.

6 You can now hang your string by pinning the ends to the wall and position your pegs at regular intervals along it to hold your Christmas cards securely in place.

Of course, you can make this card holder as long or short as you want. You could design different felt shapes and glue them on to the pegs, for example stars, simple Christmas trees and holly leaves.

Sparkly Snowflakes

Materials:

6.5 x 6.5cm (2½ x 2½in) of white felt per snowflake

6.5 x 6.5cm (2½ x 2½in) of medium-weight fusible bonding material

Small glass beads

Blue metallic embroidery cotton

Fabric glue

Tools:

Paper, fabric and embroidery scissors

Zigzag scissors

Embroidery needle

Iron

Instructions:

1 Iron the fusible bonding material on to the felt following the manufacturer's instructions.

2 Enlarge and cut out the templates on page 48. Transfer them to the back of the felt (the paper side) and cut them out using small, sharp scissors such as embroidery scissors or zigzag scissors. Peel off the paper backing.

3 Place small dots of glue on the branches of the snowflake in a geometric pattern. Let the glue dry slightly for a few seconds then place the beads on the glue, pressing them on lightly. Allow to dry thoroughly.

4 Using the full thickness of the embroidery cotton, thread it through the top of the snowflake and tie a knot to form a hanging loop of about 10cm (4in).

These snowflakes are so easy to make. Try making lots of them and attaching them together to form a garland, or make a few strands of them to hang in your window for a delicate, frosty look.

Letters to Santa

Materials:

15 x 25cm (6 x 9¾in) of white felt

20cm (7¾in) of ribbon or scraps of coloured felt and mini buttons

1 mini button for the back of the envelope

Contrasting embroidery cotton

Fabric glue

Tools:

Paper, fabric and embroidery scissors

Dressmaking pins

Embroidery needle

Paper

Pencil and ruler

Iron

Instructions:

1 On your piece of paper, draw a 15 x 25cm (6 x 9¾in) rectangle. Holding the rectangle vertically with the long edges at the side, draw a horizontal line (A) 9cm (3½in) from the bottom and another one (B) 7cm (2¾in) from the top. These will be your fold lines. Mark the middle of the top edge and draw two lines from this point to the edges of line B. This will be the flap of your envelope. Curve the point slightly. Cut out the template and transfer it to the felt, marking the fold lines with pins. Cut out the shape.

2 Fold your felt along lines A and B and iron flat to mark the folds.

3 On the front of the envelope, write the name and/or the address of the recipient with a faint pencil line. Try to keep the writing neat and regular, and centre it on the envelope. Embroider with back stitch.

4 Draw the stamp and embroider it in the same way. This could be something very simple such as a rectangle with a heart or a snowflake in it.

5 Close the sides of the envelope with blanket or overhand stitch.

6 Add small decorations to the envelope. For example, make a bow with the ribbon and stick it on to the front of the envelope with fabric glue. Alternatively, use the stocking or candy cane template on page 48 and cut one out in a different-coloured felt. Stick it on to the corner of the envelope and add a few little buttons to decorate. Add a tiny button to the point of the flap on the back. Be as creative as you want to personalise your envelope.

This envelope a great way to send letters to Santa, but it can also be used to give someone a gift voucher or some money. The envelope makes it that little bit more special and can be re-used by the recipient as a mini pouch.

Little Toy Soldier

Materials:

7 x 12cm (2¾ x 4¾in) of red felt

3 x 12cm (1¼ x 4¾in) of brown felt

9 x 16cm (3½ x 6¼in) of black felt

3 x 3cm (1¼ x 1¼in) of flesh-coloured felt

Red and black embroidery cotton

2 or 3 mini black buttons

1 red mini pompom

About 7g (¼oz) of toy filling

Fabric glue

Tools:

Paper, fabric and embroidery scissors

Pencil, paper, ruler and pair of compasses

Dressmaking pins

Embroidery needle

Iron

Sewing machine (optional)

Instructions:

1 On the piece of paper draw four rectangles: A – 12 x 4cm (4¾ x 1½in), B – 12 x 3cm (4¾ x 1¼in), C – 12 x 5cm (4¾ x 2in) and D – 12 x 7cm (4¾ x 2¾in). Also draw a circle (E) with a diameter of 3.5cm (1½in) and a square (F) of sides 2.5cm (1in). Round off the two bottom corners of the square, as this will make the face.

2 Cut out all these paper pieces and transfer them to the felt. Cut out A, C and two of E from the black felt. Cut B from the brown felt and D from the red felt. The face, F, needs to be cut from the flesh-coloured felt.

3 You now need to sew all the rectangles together. Starting from the top, place the rectangles, long sides together, in the following order: A for the hat, B for the hair, D for the jacket and C for the trousers.

4 Stitch them together by hand or using a sewing machine. If you are using hand stitching, overlap the first two rectangles by about 1cm (½in). Stitch them together with a running, back or overhand stitch. Repeat for the remaining rectangles. If you are machine stitching, place the top two rectangles wrong sides together and align the edges. Sew with a medium straight stitch. Iron the seam flat.

5 When you have sewn all the rectangles together, fold them vertically to find the centre. On this fold line, sew or glue the buttons on to the red felt.

6 For the face, with the curved edge of the flesh-coloured felt at the bottom, draw on the features with a very faint pencil line. Keep it very simple – just eyes, eyebrows and a mouth. For the eyes, use simple French knot, and for the eyebrows and mouth use back stitch.

7 Dab a little bit of glue on the back of the face and place it in the centre (above the buttons) on the brown felt, which is the hair. Leave to dry.

8 Now sew the back together. Fold the felt vertically, right sides facing in, and align all the seams so that the colours match exactly. Stitch either by hand using back stitch or with the sewing machine using a medium straight stitch.

9 Place a black circle at the bottom of the tube and pin it on all the way round. Stitch it in place with a small overhand stitch. Turn the soldier right side out and stuff with the toy filling. Place the other black circle on the top and stitch it in place with an overhand stitch. Stick the pompom on top of the hat with a little dot of glue.

Try filling the soldier with 10g (½oz) of rice instead to give him more weight. Why not make a whole army of little soldiers and use them as children's skittles? You could also put a little bell inside and sew rather than glue the face, buttons and pompom on to make a festive baby rattle – this little soldier is the perfect size for tiny hands!

Advent Garland

Materials:

35 x 45cm (13¾ x 17¾in) of white felt

35 x 45cm (13¾ x 17¾in) of red felt

22 x 27cm (8¾ x 10¾in) of green felt

2m (2yds) of ric-rac or narrow ribbon

Red and green embroidery cotton

Tools:

Paper, fabric and embroidery scissors

Pencil

Ruler

Paper

Embroidery needle

Dressmaking pins

Iron

Instructions:

1 On the piece of paper draw a 7 x 17cm (2¾ x 6¾in) rectangle and cut it out. Holding the rectangle vertically, draw a line across 10cm (4in) down from the top. This will be your fold line for each pocket.

2 Using this template, transfer the shape to the red and white felt and cut 12 of each colour. Mark the fold line with pins or a small pencil line at each end. Fold each pocket on the line and iron flat. Remove the pins.

3 Enlarge and cut out the tree template on page 46 and transfer it to the green felt. Cut out 24 trees.

4 With a very faint pencil line, draw a number on each tree from 1 to 24. Using your red embroidery cotton, stitch each number with back stitch.

5 Place one tree on the front of each pocket (the shorter side). Secure each tree in place with small overhand stitches.

6 Sew up the sides of the pockets with overhand or blanket stitch, hiding the starting knot inside.

7 Iron each little pocket flat. Line up all your pockets in the right order, keeping them very close together so they are almost touching. Take the ribbon or ric-rac and, leaving about 20cm (7¾in) at each end for the tie, pin on all the pockets along their top edge and stitch them in place with small stitches.

8 Tuck a little gift inside each pocket as a special treat for each day before Christmas.

You could add more details to this calendar if you wish. Try sewing on some beads or little bells to hang from the bottom, or use wider ribbon with a festive pattern.

Woven Felt Basket

Materials:

2 pieces of different-colour felt: 22 x 28cm (8¾ x 11in) and 18 x 28cm (7 x 11in)

Embroidery cotton

55cm (21¾in) of pompom trim

Fabric glue

55cm (21¾in) of thin, pliable craft wire

Tools:

Paper, fabric and embroidery scissors

Embroidery needle

Large piece of paper and a ruler

Fabric pen or chalk

Dressmaking pins

Iron

Instructions:

1 On the piece of paper, draw a rectangle measuring 22 x 28cm (8¾ x 11in). Inside this rectangle draw a smaller rectangle measuring 18 x 24cm (7¼ x 9½in), leaving a 2cm (¾in) frame. Cut out both rectangles and transfer the frame to one of the pieces of felt. Do not cut yet!

2 On this piece of felt, along the longer edges of the inner rectangle, make a small mark every 2cm (¾in). Draw parallel lines to join the marks, 11 in total. Also draw in the lines down either side of the inner rectangle, making 13 parallel lines altogether.

3 With small, sharp scissors such as embroidery scissors, cut along these 13 parallel lines, taking care to leave the 2cm (¾in) frame completely uncut. You will then have a piece of felt with 13 slits cut in it but no felt removed. This will be the main structure of your basket.

4 Take your other piece of felt and cut 9 strips of 28 x 2cm (11 x ¾in).

5 Now simply weave the strips of felt into your frame. To do this, take your large piece of felt and position it with the slits lying vertically. Lay one strip across the felt with the upper edge aligned with the tops of the slits, and pin one end to the edge of the frame. Weave it through all the way to the other side, then pin the other end in place. Weave the other strips as regularly as you can until you reach the bottom of the slits.

6 Glue all the ends where you have put pins, then remove the pins and leave to dry.

7 You now need to shape your basket. Measure 6cm (2¼in) from the edge on all four sides. Mark with pins. Fold the longer sides along the marked line and iron in place. Leave these sides folded flat and fold the two shorter sides. Iron these flat too. This will have marked your corners.

You could swap the pompoms for a beautiful embroidered braid or a beaded trimming.

8 Place your felt basket on a flat surface, and lift both long sides and one short side. As you do so, two points will be formed at the corners, pointing outwards. Match the edges and pin each corner to hold. Repeat on the other short side.

9 You should now have a rectangular basket with four points sticking out at the corners. You simply need to fold these back, flat on the sides. Match the edges and stitch in place with a few overhand stitches. Iron the sides.

10 Straighten your piece of wire. Start stitching it around the top edge of your basket with an overhand stitch. Go all the way round and trim the wire to size. Make sure the wire is bent around each corner and straight along the edges.

11 Place a thin line of glue along the outer top edge and stick your pompom trim all the way round.

Winter Owls

Materials:

24 x 11cm (9½ x 4¼in) of brown or white felt for the body and wings

3 x 6cm (1¼ x 2¼in) of contrasting felt for the eyes

20 x 2cm (7¾ x ¾in) of red felt for the scarf

Scrap of brown or black felt for the beak and pupils

2 x 2cm (¾in) diameter wooden buttons for the eyes (optional)

15–20cm (6–7¾in) of thin ribbon or string

Embroidery cotton

About 8g (½oz) of toy filling

Tools:

Paper, fabric and embroidery scissors

Embroidery needle

Instructions:

1 Enlarge the templates on page 46 and cut them out. Transfer the shapes to the felt and cut two body pieces and two wings from the large piece of felt, and one beak and two eyes from the smaller pieces of felt.

2 Take the long piece of red felt and, with your embroidery scissors, cut little fringes along both ends. Do not cut them too thin or they will tear and fall off. About 5–8mm (¼in) wide is ideal.

3 For the button eyes, lay the felt circles on the front body piece with the wooden buttons on top. Secure them to the body with a few stitches through the buttonholes. For the felt eyes, place the felt circles on the front body piece and stitch them in place with long straight stitches starting from the centre and radiating outwards. Cut a small circle of brown or black felt for each pupil, about 0.5–1cm (¼–½in) diameter, and stitch in the centre of the eye. Finish with a French knot.

4 Place the beak just below the eyes and sew it in place with a few overhand stitches.

5 Take your length of ribbon and fold it in half. This will be the hanging loop. Place it at the top of the head on the wrong side of the back body piece. Make a couple of small stitches to secure it. Do not cut your thread. Put the front piece on top of the back piece, wrong sides together, with the ends of the hanging loop sandwiched between the two. Sew all the way round with blanket or overhand stitch. Stuff the owl with toy filling before closing it completely.

6 Place the wings on the sides of the owl about half-way down and sew them along the top with a few overhand stitches.

7 Tie the scarf around the neck of the owl to keep it nice and warm.

You could fill these owls with herbs or spices such as dried lavender or cinnamon to fill your home with a festive aroma.

Pretty Felt Pot

Materials:

55 x 20cm (21¾ x 7¾in) of red or white felt for the outer part of the pot

42 x 20cm (16½ x 7¾in) of contrasting felt for the lining (I used red with the white pot and green with the red pot)

Embroidery cotton

42 x 20cm (16½ x 7¾in) of medium-weight fusible bonding material

30cm (11¾in) of ribbon

Tools:

Paper, fabric and embroidery scissors

Embroidery needle

Large piece of paper

Pencil, ruler and pair of compasses

Iron

Dressmaking pins

Instructions:

1 On the piece of paper, draw a rectangle of 41 x 19cm (16¼ x 7½in) and a circle of diameter 12.5cm (5in). Cut these out. Lay the rectangle with the long edges running horizontally, and draw a line 6cm (2¼in) from the top edge. On this line, mark points at 8, 16, 24, 32 and 40cm (or 3⅛, 6¼, 9½, 12⅝ and 15¾in) from the left-hand edge. On the top edge mark points at 4, 12, 20, 28 and 36cm (1⅝, 4¾, 7⅞, 11 and 14⅛in). Link these points to create a large zigzag pattern. There will be 1cm (½in) left on the right-hand side, which will become the seam allowance. Cut along the zigzag line to create the five points.

2 Take the larger piece of felt and cut it into two pieces: 42 x 20cm (16½ x 7¾in) and 13 x 20cm (5 x 7¾in). On the smaller of these two pieces, draw around your circle template and cut it out. Put to one side.

3 On the larger piece, decide on the pattern you wish to embroider and draw it with a faint pencil line. Bear in mind that the long edges will be at the top and bottom of the pot, and that the top of the pattern should be at least 10cm (4in) from the top. Simple designs work very well: I have used a double line of running stitch with French knots on the white pot, and simple stars made with long stitches and French knots on the red pot. Embroider the design using a contrasting coloured thread.

4 When you have finished your embroidery, iron the fusible bonding material on to the back of the felt. Leave it to cool and transfer the template you made in step 1 on to the paper side. Cut out the shape.

5 Peel off the paper and lay the felt, sticky side down, on top of the contrasting piece of lining felt. Iron on both sides to bond the two pieces together. Leave to cool and trim off the lining felt to match the outer felt perfectly. Make sure all the points are trimmed neatly.

6 Roll your double felt into a cylinder with the points at the top. Tuck the extra 1cm (½in) of felt on the right-hand side under the other edge. Pin then sew the seam using straight stitch.

Try sewing small jingle bells on the end of each point to add to the festive look. If you are using your pot as a gift box, perhaps make a matching tag (see page 24) or embroider on the recipient's name to make it even more special. The pot also makes a pretty storage box for jewellery, hair accessories or other little treasures.

7 Take the circle of felt you cut in step 2 and sew it on to the base of your cylinder with overhand stitch.

8 Your little pot is now finished and ready to use. You can place a gift inside, such as a jar of home-made jam or some chocolates, and tie the ribbon around it just below the points; curl the points outwards, as in the picture, to make a pretty festive gift. Alternatively, fold the points down, ironing the fold flat so that it stays in shape, and use your pot to hold a wine bottle or other treats on the Christmas table.

Christmas Angels

Materials:

10 x 12cm (4 x 4¾in) of pale blue or white felt for the body

10 x 8cm (4 x 3¼in) of white or red felt for the wings

2 x 2cm (¾ x ¾in) of flesh-coloured felt for the face

Embroidery cotton: either silver metallic or in a contrasting colour to decorate the robe and sew the angel together; brown or black for the face

About 5g (¼oz) of toy filling

Tools:

Paper, fabric and embroidery scissors

Embroidery needle

Pencil

Fabric glue

Instructions:

1 Enlarge the templates on page 47 and cut them out. Transfer the shapes to the felt and cut two body pieces, one wing piece and one face.

2 Draw the features on the face with a faint pencil line. Keep it simple – a simple, curved mouth and dots for eyes work well. You can also add a suggestion of hair to the top of the face, as on the blue angel opposite. Use back stitch to embroider the features.

3 Decorate the front of the body with a few stars made with simple straight stitches in a contrasting colour. Use the silver metallic thread for added sparkle.

4 Sew all the way round the wings with blanket stitch. Again, use either a contrasting colour or silver metallic thread. This not only looks pretty, but will help to strengthen them too.

5 Position the pair of wings on the back body piece and attach them with a line of straight stitches going down the centre. Use the same thread as you used around the outside.

6 Cut an 18cm (7in) length of cotton thread and fold it in half to form a hanging loop. Knot the ends and place the knot on the wrong side of the back body piece, at the top. Place the front body piece on top, wrong sides facing, and sew them together with a simple overhand stitch. Use either a contrasting thread or the silver metallic thread. Stuff your angel with toy filling before closing it completely.

7 Glue the face on to the front of the head with a few dots of fabric glue.